How Do I Do This Thing Called Life?

An Everyday Person's Guide to Finding True Happiness

Brooke Barnes

To my fiancé, Scott.

Thank you for always sticking by my side and encouraging me in all my pursuits. You never doubt my ability to do what I set out to do, even when things look pretty bleak.

You are my person. Thank you for everything.

I will love you forever.

To my children: Adrienne, Davis, Emma, and Scarlet.

For every time I have failed you so far, there will be a hundred where I will go above and beyond for all of you. You four remain a source of constant inspiration for me to continue pushing through all of the tough stuff in life to do better for you.

You will always be my babies.

I love you all so much.

CONTENTS

INTRODUCTION:

So, what are we going to look at in this guide? What advice can I possibly provide to you with my history? Well, the short answer is:

A LOT!

I have experience in most of the tough situations that someone may have to face at some point or another in their life. And all of that experience has given me an understanding of the world and how things work that I never could have imagined having before.

A lot of the experts out there do not truly have first-hand knowledge of what it takes to create a true change in your own happiness. They have not faced tough situations themselves. They have gotten all their information from third party accounts or studies or some other source. They do not speak from their own hearts about the advice they are giving.

So, I am excited to share this knowledge with you

that has all been gained first-hand through my own experience.

First, we are going to talk about loyalty. This topic needed to be a standalone section of the book because, while it is not a lengthy section by any means, it is highly important to the way that you see and value yourself in your everyday life.

In our second section, we are going to cover a couple of topics about your professional self and how to enhance and protect it. These will be keeping your own work product designs, continuous learning, and overall, just preparing for the worst while working towards the best. Put yourself first in everything you do!

Our third section is going to be much longer and cover topics in the personal life sector. If you consider these tips and incorporate them in your daily life (and I mean really use them and not say that you will and never do it) then I can promise you that you will feel better about your life situations. We are going to look at spending habits, hobbies, relationships, and more. This is my favorite section of this book as it talks about things that we can do every day to increase our own abilities to be happy in a genuine way.

And finally, the last section of this guide will be the shortest of all. It is going to be the key takeaway from the guide. There is one simple lesson that all the tips in this book revolve around. Put it at the center of everything in your life and watch how things evolve.

So, let's jump in and get started!

PREFACE:

So, let me backtrack and restart by saying I am not an expert by any means. I am not a psychologist or a self-help guru. I am a regular, average, everyday person. I do not hold a degree of any kind. I was not born into a wealthy family that helped give me any advantages.

I have faced my share of struggles throughout my adult life. I have lost jobs that I loved with a second's notice. I have gone through a foreclosure on my first home. I have had my car repossessed, more than once. I have consistently lived paycheck to paycheck, and rarely ever had substantial savings built up. I have been in debt up to my eyeballs that I am still working to pay down (we are all young and dumb at some point in our lives and it comes back to haunt us!). I have found myself short on money for bills or food more than once.

Does all this mean that I am a failure?

Absolutely Not! It means I have had to pick myself up and start things again!

Does this mean I am not qualified to give out advice

to other people? Absolutely Not! I believe it makes me uniquely qualified to provide advice and support to others in these situations.

You do not have to be an expert to help someone in any way, shape, or form. Giving advice and tips is an easy way to pass on knowledge from your own life experiences to help make the journey slightly less treacherous for someone else. And once you have started implementing these tips and see results for yourself, that is when you want to share them with others.

I am laying this out in the hopes that it gives you some insight into the author of this book. I want it to be clear that this advice is coming from actual life experience and not what every other self-proclaimed 'Expert' out there has rehashed over and over.

With all of that said, this book will give the tips I have begun to implement in my own life and the reasons why. My belief is that these life tips will genuinely increase your own happiness as they have done for me. Instead of focusing on superficial items in your life, these tips will help get to the root of things that may be causing you to feel like you do not measure up or that you are lacking in some way. And if you make it through this guide and feel that there is nothing you need to change in your own life to make yourself happier, well, I wish you the absolute best of luck! That is the level of self-awareness that I am working to achieve.

However, if you are like me and feel that there are

many areas in your life in which you can improve, then these tips should stick in your brain the next time you come across a situation where they will be useful.

That is the entire intent behind this guide. Am I an expert?

No.

Do you need expert advice to be happy?

No.

What is needed are small tips and tricks that you can use over time to boost your situation. I would like to provide some of my favorites now. I truly hope you see as much of a benefit in them as I do.

The reason that I decided to write this guide was that I was recently laid off with no notice. And I realized that even though I no longer had a job or an income, that I was still happy.

How many people can really say that they would feel this way if something like this would have happened to them?

I want this guide to serve as a 'Prepper Handbook' for others. It will show you ways to make yourself genuinely happy based on what has worked for me personally. This is not based on research or studies of any kind. This advice is coming from my own life experiences and may not suit everyone. But I believe it will be highly beneficial to others.

PART I – LOYALTY: WHO GETS IT AND WHO DOESN'T

BLIND LOYALTY TO YOUR EMPLOYER? DROP IT FAST!

A lot of people will tell you that loyalty is something that is earned over time, like trust. Or that you should always be loyal to an employer just because they sign your paycheck. This may not be the worst advice; however, it is different from what I am about to tell you. Are you ready to hear it? Okay, here it is: Loyalty is for family and friends. Not employers.

Read that again. Let it sink in. Really think about it. In your daily life, who is there when you are in trouble? Who comes to the rescue if something bad happens? Who checks in on you when you are sick or someone you love passes away?

Your family and your friends are there. All the time. They are there for your ups and downs. They are there for all the beginnings, middles, and ends in your life. Birthdays, holidays, anniversaries, major life changes, and everything in between.

Now think about the company that you work for. Do they mail you a template birthday card every year? Yeah, that is 'nice' I guess. But there is no thought in that, and no genuine care being shown. Do you get the standard vacation and pay increases for your work anniversary every year? Again, it is a nice perk. But does it show any caring on the employer's part? Absolutely not.

These employer 'perks' are just that. They are in place for every employee. There is no specification based on you as a person. Meaning there is no true loyalty. Some companies may do well with recognition and employee rewards. However, most do them just as a way to keep employees, so they are not constantly hiring and having a large percentage of turnover. It is not because they genuinely care about the people working for them.

A lot of you may be thinking "Brooke, what are you talking about? My employer is like a second family. My boss loves me, and we chat about our families and things every day.". That is all well and good. But it still will not stop them from cutting you if they face losses or a downturn of any kind. Being prepared for this and understanding that a company has no obligation to you is the first step in understanding how to make yourself happy. Having a mentality of "That would never happen to me." is a very dangerous thing, especially in times like the current where we are seeing a large number of layoffs weekly across industries. You should always be aware that it can happen to you, no matter what your position or what company you work for.

All the organizations out there will scrutinize you when you apply for being a 'job-hopper'. However, they do not consider their own parts in that. Organizations release employees with no thought as to how it will affect their work history. When you are laid off, end a short-term contract, etc., it still makes it appear as though you did not intend to stay long-term. Do not let the fear of being labeled a job-hopper stop you from considering new opportunities if that is what is best for you and your own situation. You do not owe it to your current employer to stay just because you are already there. Organizations also do not consider what prompted you to make the decision to leave your previous employers. Maybe the culture was awful. Maybe the job was completely different from what was described during your hiring process. Maybe you got started and realized that you really, really dislike the work. The reason does not matter. You do not have to stay in a job that makes you unhappy. Regardless of how long you have been there. One of our rights as people is the right to the pursuit of happiness. This includes being happy professionally.

Now back to loyalty to a company. At the end of the day, if your company suffers, will they consider you as an individual before making any decisions, such as whom to lay off? Or will they make cuts based on salary and tenure alone? Will they look at your contributions to the company? Will they look at your family situation? Will they take any factors from your personal life into consideration?

I personally just faced this situation a few days before beginning this book. My employer called me and said due to losing a client that my position was being eliminated at the end of the day. And I wasn't the only person affected by this cut within the company.

My whole world was shifted in a second. I had been with the organization for just under a year. I felt like my bosses and coworkers were an extended family. They had always treated everyone so well. We had the most amazing 'perks' working for the company. Our whole company talked like family and knew what was happening in each other's lives, both personally and professionally.

And then... it was over.

Like many other organizations, the moment there was a sign of possible decline, they made the decision to cut people with no thought of how it would impact their lives.

Did they consider the amount of work I had been putting in before making that decision? No. If they had, they would have considered that just at the end of the previous week, I was recognized for having the most calls in the organization for the entire previous year (the other employee who was released at the same time tied with me for this recognition). They would have considered that I had consistently been recognized for sending the most outreach messages in the organization month to month.

If they had considered any personal factors, they would have considered my family, my bills, and how immediately losing my income could affect my entire life. They would have considered my fiancé, who is battling cancer and is close to remission but not quite there, and the added stress this situation would cause not just myself, but my fiancé as well. Not to mention the possible lack of funds due to the loss of my income to make it to his treatments and visits.

They would have considered that I had a car payment and that losing my job could in turn also cause me to lose my car. But my position was eliminated with no notice and no offer of severance. My insurance was eliminated on the same day as my employment. Not only was I cast out but so was my family.

I am going a little deep with this because I was the typical loyal and devoted employee. I did not just work my scheduled hours. I would send outreaches at 7 am or 7 pm. I would work on the weekends, reviewing applications and sending out more messages. I personally worked on extra ways to be more productive, creating and updating my own tracking methods to measure metrics and performance. I found new features on tools that we used as an organization and even led training on those features and how implementing them has increased my own production.

And still, when the challenging times hit, my company felt it was better to immediately jump to eliminating my role. When push comes to shove, a company is loyal to nobody but the company. So, you need to do the same. Be loyal to yourself and the ones you love. Do not give unquestioned loyalty to an organization. Because they will not give the same to you.

Now, I would like to clarify that I am not saying to change jobs every six months just so you can get a higher income or a change of scenery. That is not at all the point.

I am saying that you should allow yourself to be open to options that would give your life value an increase.

Maybe in your current role, you are lacking customer interaction. All your work is with internal employees. But you have a true passion for working with customers from previous roles and really want to move back into that type of work. If you allow yourself the opportunity to connect with organizations and recruiters who may reach out to you, you could discover a new position that will include customer interaction and give you what you have been missing in your current role.

This has happened to me more than once. I was working in a role that I had thought had a good career path laid out. There were clear steps that I would be taking, along with a timeline, to continue moving up until I reached a Branch Manager level role.

The first time, my company went through a restructuring that completely obliterated my career path. There would now be at least one lateral move required before making a progression forward along my chosen path. This no longer aligned with what I wanted as it lengthened my process by at least a year. And I was chomping at the bit to get moving forward in my career. So, I began entertaining other roles.

The next time that it happened was similar to the restructuring issue. This time, I had been led to believe my compensation structure upon promotion would be much higher than what it actually would be. Mind you, money is not everything to me. As long as my family can live comfortably, then I am happy. However, the amount that was laid out during my hiring process was significantly higher than the actual amount discussed down the road. The amount truly on the table for this promotion would have been less than I had made as an entry-level recruiter with another company.

To me that was unfathomable.

With the extra amount of work and responsibility that I would be undertaking and to know that I was not even making as much as most recruiters? I could not stand behind an organization like that that undervalued their employees and blatantly showed it with the salaries that they offered.

Now, about the same time that I was making this discovery about the organization that I was working for, a previous coworker reached out to me about a new organization. This coworker was currently at that organization and loving it! At first, I told the coworker that I was not really looking for anything new as I had just moved into my current organization about two months prior to this.

However, the more I considered what she had said was offered with that organization, the more it sounded like a change I truly needed to consider. So, I reached back out to the coworker and said I would like to learn more. They helped me set up a call with the hiring manager, coached me before the call, and basically helped everything to fall into place to get an amazing offer to join the organization.

And I said yes.

I decided to make a change after just under three months at my current organization because I knew it was not right for me. I knew that I would never be genuinely happy in the role that I had because, in my mind, the organization that I was with did not allow employees to be compensated at a fair rate for the work they were tasked with.

So, when you are thinking about your loyalty to your current company, there are definitely many factors to consider. In the end, you must make the best decision for yourself and your family. Do not let anything that an employer has 'done for you' influence your decision. Again, loyalty is for friends and family. Not employers.

PTO – USE OR USE IT, THERE IS NO LOSE IT OPTION

My next piece of personal advice: take your PTO. All of it. Do not bank it for a just-in-case scenario.

When your PTO resets for the year, plan out your major trips (if you have any) and how much PTO time you will have left. Schedule your doctor's visits and such. Then allocate your remaining PTO days every so often to give you an additional break from work. Take a three-day weekend now and then. Take a day off mid-week just because. Take the week of your birthday off and just sit around the house in your PJs reading a few good books.

It does not matter when or what the reason. Use your PTO. Do not let yourself feel guilty for using your PTO either. PTO is earned. Yes, some organizations give you a bank of PTO to draw from and others have accrual-based PTO programs. Either way, your PTO is earned, and you deserve to take that time. Do not let your PTO expire. You know, the old 'Use It or Lose It' policy. Do NOT become a victim of this policy.

As I said, PTO is earned by you and when you do not use it and don't get it paid out, you are basically giving something that you earned back to the organization that you are working for. Meaning that the value of your total compensation package has decreased. So basically, you allowed yourself to be shorted on income that you should have received because of what? You were nervous to take time off and look bad? You felt you were too busy at work to be able to take time off without falling behind?

That is definitely not how things should feel between you and your employer regarding your ability to take PTO. Keep the loyalty for yourself and your family, remember? Everybody needs a chance to reset from time to time. And that is nothing to be ashamed of or embarrassed by.

Make sure all your work bases are covered (i.e., out-of-office responses, somebody chosen to cover emergency situations that would typically fall on your desk, etc.), and then let yourself disconnect for that hard-earned time off.

And make sure you are fully unplugged if you are taking your PTO. Do not check your emails, voicemails, or any other types of messages or programs you typically work with daily. PTO is "paid time off", with the key words being 'time off'. Do not do work unless you are getting paid for it. You are not a volunteer for the company you work for so do not act like one (again loyalty is for your family and friends, not the company you work for).

I am personally horrible at following this. I consistently checked my work email on my phone, even on my time off, whether it was time outside of my normal working hours or PTO. I would go through emails, respond to messages, and even boot up my laptop to submit new candidates, review orders coming through, and even add notes to files that were not urgent.

These tasks could have easily waited until I returned to the office. Or I could have asked someone else to complete some of them for me. But I did not want anyone to think I was a slacker. I wanted to make sure everything got done, and that it got done right. I wanted to own my processes from start to finish with nobody else getting into them.

What I realize now is that this did not help me in any way. I still got laid off. My work ethic did not make a difference. My personality did not make a difference. My drive did not make a difference. My work during my PTO time did not make a difference. My loyalty to my company did not make a difference.

Looking back now, I should have fully unplugged. I should not have taken working PTO. I should have taken true, out of office, do not try to reach me, PTO. So that is my advice to you. Do not let your PTO go to waste. Take your time off. And take it all.

When is the last time you took a day off (not including calling in sick)? If it has been more than a month, schedule a day off ASAP if you have the PTO stocked up. If it has been more than two months, schedule yourself a four-day weekend. If it has been more than three months, then schedule yourself a whole week off. Allow yourself to realize it is okay. Feel good about your time off. Enjoy the time. And make sure you are not giving something away that is yours.

PART II – GROWING YOUR PROFESSIONAL SELF

KEEP LEARNING!

I am sure after reading that last section, you have a few thoughts going through your mind. These may range from worry about being laid off, trying to figure out the last time you had a day off, and a whole mess of things in between. What I would like to cover now is one of my favorite pieces of advice for disaster planning in your career. And the reason it works so well is that is the answer to many problems and questions you may face in the professional world.

How do I get the promotion I want?

How do I move into a new career industry?

How do I make myself recession-proof, marketable, and valuable to any future employer?

The simple answer is to keep growing! First, do NOT stop learning because you are comfortable in your current position. Keep learning new skills and technologies that could be used in similar roles or higher positions. Learn a new dashboard and visualization program. Learn a new programming language. Learn a new formula for Excel. Just learn and keep learning.

For example, as a Technical Recruiter, I have mostly worked with one ATS system, Bullhorn. I absolutely love this system and its features. However, not all companies use this same ATS. So, when I am looking for my next role, I can market myself easier to companies looking for someone with experience on this specific ATS, but not with others.

A simple fix for this is, of course, to learn another ATS system. But how do I teach myself a new system? Where do I even start? There are tons of resources out there to teach yourself new skills.

My favorite currently is LinkedIn Learning. Yes, you need to have a subscription to access the courses and training. However, in my opinion, the subscription pays for itself with the breadth of knowledge available at your fingertips. And each course awards a certification upon completion with validation credentials. This is your showcase to your current and future employers that you take the initiative to learn new skills and are highly valuable to the organization.

Another great place to learn new skills is Coursera. You can purchase a plan for a year and have access to all their courses (which also include certifications at the end of each course). While the cost is greater upfront than other methods, there is tremendous value in this type of subscription plan as you can save a lot in the long run by paying for a full year of access upfront. A lot of their courses are led by instructors from accredited universities and large companies you may be familiar with, such as AWS and Google.

And these are just two that I have personally used. There are hundreds, if, not more, of other companies out there offering online learning as well!

Now maybe you are like me and are more of a thrifty learner. These subscription services that I have mentioned do have a cost associated with them. However, there are ways to do the courses for free! If you just want access to the material and not the certification after completion, you can enroll as an auditor of the course and access all the course materials for free!!! That means you get all the knowledge the same way you would if you paid for the course. The only thing missing is the certification. Build out some of your own projects using what you learn and create a portfolio and the certification will not be necessary to show to a prospective employer anyway!

Another thrift way (I am all about the thrift vibes!) is to check out bookstores for how-to guides for new skills in your industry. Even better, get used copies at book resellers! They are still great quality books at an even cheaper price. You can go at your own pace, highlight, make notes, and review the readings over and over to make sure you truly grasp the material. Self-study books also often come with projects laid out in them so you can practice your new skills and make sure you have a thorough understanding of exactly what you would be using them for.

Another great method for continuous learning is online webinars. When I scroll through my LinkedIn, I am constantly seeing new webinars being offered in all different areas. I personally set a goal to view one new webinar per week, to keep myself fresh and gain different insight from leaders in my industry. I bet if you look at your feed you can find a webinar that looks interesting to you within five minutes of scrolling. Add it to your calendar and boom! You are learning!

Whatever method you choose, be it online learning, books, or some other method, just do it. Be a continuous learner and you will keep yourself relevant and marketable in the workforce. You may even find those skills you have been lacking that have been holding you back from your next promotion!

PROTECT YOUR WORK PRODUCTS, DESIGNS, AND IDEAS

You should always make sure that any work product you produce on your own is stored as a blank copy on your personal systems.

Let me explain.

Say you are tasked with creating a new dashboard for your company. You need to include all open positions that you are recruiting for (I will use a lot of recruiting examples since that is my industry). You also need to include the worksite requirements, type of role, pay information, candidate names, and the status of any active candidate at any given time. Now, you take all the requirements and build out an amazing dashboard. You add color coding for easy eye reference of candidate status. You add formatting so your dashboard auto-updates when certain selections are made. You have drop-down menus and every other amazing feature you could think of.

You present your new dashboard to your manager and they love it!

They implement the dashboard for use by your team. Some time passes and you are let go.

Did you save a blank copy to your own computer and your own files? So how will you show your next potential employer your creative ability to solve problems and innovate new methods of pipelining and tracking project status?

Keeping a blank copy means you are not taking privileged company information with you. And it gives you items to add to your portfolio of projects you have managed and completed.

Do you see where I am going with this?

It all comes back to the loyalty section. Make sure you are loyal to yourself and keeping yourself marketable for that just in case instance. Every additional item that you create and can have your name on is an extra addition to the portfolio that your next potential employer will be reviewing. And that one project you forgot to save could just be the one thing that would have landed you your dream job.

UPDATE YOUR RESUME.... ALL THE TIME!

Always, always keep your resume updated.

Did you just start a new job?

Add it to your resume now. Add your start date. Add your job title and the company. Add a detailed description based on what you know about the role so far.

Then, as you work in the role longer, go back and update that job description to include more duties and skills you are using in your day-to-day. Add any accomplishments you hit while in that role.

And for your own sanity, add any metrics that you can as you get them (for instance, you consistently managed twenty-five to forty-five open client requisition orders at any given time, you had an average of five new candidates start positions each week, etc.).

Got a promotion? You guessed it. Add it to your resume.

Add the effective date of the promotion. Add your new job title and updated description and responsibilities of the role.

Do not let yourself get behind on this crucial step in a job search. If you leave your role for any reason, you will start slow in your job search because now you must update your resume and try to add every detail needed for a new employer to see your value. Keeping it updated as you go saves so much time and effort if that crucial moment of looking for a new role springs up unexpectedly.

Under this same concept, make sure you are including all new courses completed and certifications obtained. You really don't want to lag on this if, like me, you are constantly enrolled in learning courses that grant certifications upon completion. You don't want to find yourself trying to remember all the certifications you have completed in the past three years when you are trying to get back into the job search game.

When you are updating your resume, please make it as simple as possible.

Unless you are in a creative/design field, you do not need a ridiculously formatted resume with multi-colored designs and such.

The same goes for personal information. Keep it limited on your resume. You should have your name and contact info. That is it. You do not need a photo on your resume. You do not need your interests and hobbies on your resume.

Personally, when I am recruiting for roles, I find that resumes that come through that are overly formatted with pictures and different fonts and blocking are distracting.

I much prefer a simple layout where I can quickly find the sections I need to review before reaching out to an applicant.

The sections I look atare limited. I review the summary, work experience, and education. Everything I need to make an informed decision about a candidate should be included in these three sections.

An even bigger piece is: do these sections match up? If you give a great description of who you are as a professional in your summary, it should be reflected in your work experience. If it is not, then you need o do a thorough resume review and some rewriting.

You want to include all tools you used in your work experience descriptions. An employer needs to be able to look at your work experience accomplishments and quickly reference what tools you were using to achieve those accomplishments.

Having a skills section on your resume is great, but if the skills are not reflected directly in your experience, then it may be assumed by someone reading your resume that you do not have any true experience with that skill.

For example, back to my own experience, I have used one ATS system for the majority of my recruiting experience. But that is not the only system I have experience with. So while I may showcase that specific ATS experience under relevant roles and in my resume summary, I need to make sure that the other ATS systems I have used are also listed under their respective roles. This shows a potential employer that I am able to learn multiple systems and may already possess the skill needed for their available role.

Along with my ATS system used, I should also be listing out other tools used, such as MS Office, Google Workspace, CRM systems, background vendor systems, payroll processing software, etc.

Your job descriptions on your resume are your place to shine from your previous roles. It is up to you to write something that will draw a potential employer in and make them want to learn more about your experience.

They want to see your highlights. They want to see your accomplishments. They want to see your toolkit that you have built over your career. And this is how you present all of that to them!

Make your resume work for you. Keep it updated. Optimize it. Have multiple versions if you are interested in different types of roles so that you summary matches up with each role you may be applying to.

I have different versions of my resume for recruiting, payroll, and HR positions. My summaries are all tailored differently based on what is most important to showcase for eah type of role. Speaking in my summary about sourcing and ATS experience is not really relevant to what I need to showcase to land a new role in payroll.

Going back to my statement from earlier, keep it simple but make it standout by the content you include in your resume.

TAKE ON ADDITIONAL RESPONSIBILITY IN YOUR CURRENT ROLE

Updating your resume consistently also allows you to review your career progress so far and see where you want to go and what your next step may be to get there.

Are you a recruiter like me but you are wanting to move into an Account Executive or Client Manager role? Reading through your resume will allow you to compare your own experience against standard requirements for these roles and see what you may need to start working on now to reach that next career step.

Maybe you need to work on having more client interaction. If your employer allows it, you can request to hop on new order calls with hiring managers at the client site. This way, you start building a relationship with the client, and you can begin to see what the next role for you entails.

Ask if you can also be involved in discussions on candidates submitted. Speak with your Account Manager or Client Manager about their duties. Explain that you are interested in moving into that type of role and that you would like to start learning what it involves.

Most employers will see this as you taking the extra initiative and will at least allow some shadowing so that you can get an idea of what may be in store for you down the road. And then you can see if there is anything that you may be able to take over in addition to your current duties.

Now, please keep in mind, if you are not a solid performer in your current role, it may not be the best idea to ask about taking on additional responsibilities. Your employer might be worried that you would start dropping the ball in your regular duties with which you are already struggling. In this case, I would suggest working to improve your performance in your current role first. If there is some metric you are not hitting, work a little harder each week to see if you can improve that. If you are having an issue turning candidates who are submitted into interview requests or offers for hire, go back and see what your successful placements have in common and try to redirect your search efforts for additional candidates to match those common win factors.

Once you have brought your performance in your

current role up, then you should approach your manager about learning new skills and trying to take on some additional duties. Once you start working on these new duties on a regular basis, guess what is next?

Add them to your resume! Make a little bullet point about additional duties taken on after requesting more responsibility in this role. This will stand out to future prospective employers and really solidify that you are a candidate that can manage extra work, and even welcomes it!

NETWORK, NETWORK, NETWORK... THEN NETWORK SOME MORE!

You should always network, network, network. My number one go-to for this is LinkedIn. Send ten to fifteen new connection requests per day. Build up your contacts. Branch out and connect with people who may not be in the same role or industry as you are currently, but maybe they are in something closely related that you might consider moving into in the future.

Going back to being a technical recruiter again for another example, I have spent time sending connection requests to recruiters for other industries like finance, HR, operations, and more. Again, this has built up my network much larger than just people in my own standard professional circle.

These added connections allow me to view articles on LinkedIn that I would not have seen before. I have more webinars showing up in my feed in which I am interested. I see more viewpoints on things I could be doing to improve my own skills and marketability for future roles.

When I received the news that my role was eliminated, I was able to go to my LinkedIn and make a post that I was looking for work. This post was then shared with my entire network. Connections in my network reacted to my post, not only showing support but that simple 'Like' or 'Support' reaction then allowed my post to be shown to connections in their network. My post was also reshared by some of my connections, again, instantly adding visibility of the post to connections in their networks.

Hopefully, you can see how this would be valuable if you are suddenly finding yourself looking for a new role with no idea where to start. You can go to your network, make a simple post, and then step back and take a breath while your network begins working for you.

After this post is up and circulating, start working on additional resume updates (including the end date of your last employer!), creating an outline of positions you would like to try to apply for, making your LinkedIn profile more marketable to employers, and making sure your online portfolio is updated with all projects that you would like to showcase.

Doing things in this way allows your profile to start being seen by hiring managers, without the stress of having to have an updated resume already submitted and a formal portfolio sent over. They may see your profile and look through your information there and go ahead and reach out to you. Or you may get messages from your connections with links to jobs that you may be interested in.

Once you are ready, you can come back and start taking the next steps from the outreach and feedback that you receive from your network!

Now I am not saying try to make your network do everything for you by any means. And this is not a guarantee that something will come out of it. But it can be a very large help in guiding you toward your next role. If that time comes and you are looking for your next career stop, remember that your network can be more than just prospects as well.

Find a job that sounds amazing? See who the job poster is and connect with them!! Add a note to your connection request stating that you just applied for their open role and would love to connect and discuss more details. One extra step that gives you a leg up over your competition for the role.

You can also view the company page of a prospective employer to get more details on what types of roles they currently have available, what the average tenure is for employees, and how much growth they have seen. You will see links to their company website, where you will find even more valuable data about their company history. And, you can look under the people tab on LinkedIn to view people that are listed as working for that employer, filter by the type of job you are looking for, and then compare your own resume and profile with their experience to see if you may also be a good match for that position. This will also show you if you should do some editing of your page to word things or showcase things a little differently.

PART III – GROWING YOUR PERSONAL SELF

AUTOMATE YOUR BILLS

This one is an easy decision. But a lot of people still are not aware that they can do this. Or have just chosen not to set this up yet.

And my question is: Why?

Do they not yet know the benefits of automatic bill payments? Do they think it will cost them more overall? Do they not use electronic payments because they do not want their account information on file online?

None of these are good enough reasons to miss out on potential savings on your bills and keep yourself ahead on payments.

But what are the benefits of automatic bill pay?

Never be late with your payment again! In my opinion, this is the most important benefit because on time payments mean good reporting to the credit bureaus. Maybe even pay a little extra each month if you can, without really even trying hard! By setting up your own auto payments, you can also set the amount that you would like to pay and how often. Meaning if your monthly amount due on a bill is

$175, and you set up a weekly auto payment of $50, then you will pay an extra $25 a month on that bill without having to think about it.

Depending on the type of bill, that could cut down on the total interest amount that you will be repaying over the life of the payments. Savings, yes, please! If you are someone who has never set up an automatic bill payment before, it can seem daunting to try and figure out how to do it.

My best piece of advice for this is to first look into doing auto bill pay directly from your bank account. This option is typically available to you through your online or mobile banking platform. You will need all of the information for the account that you will be making payments to, including the company/entity name, address, phone number, and the account number that you will be paying on.

Once you have added the account for payments to your bank account, you will be able to schedule automatic payments for the frequency and amount of your choosing. This is definitively the easiest option as you can manage all your auto-pay bills in one place.

As an added bonus, you may already track your bank account like a hawk (I know I check my on several times a day in my bank's mobile app) so you can easily hop over to see if there are any automatic payments scheduled in the next few days to see if you have the extra money right now to grab that latte while you are out and about!

Now, there are times when an account will not be

eligible for autopay directly through your bank, and the circumstances for that differ from bank to bank and account to account. However, if you find that one of your bills is tied to an ineligible account, there is another simple way to set up automatic payments. Go directly to that company's website or mobile app (whichever you already use for payments) and select the option for making a payment. Usually, this is the menu where you can find an option for setting up recurring payments or scheduling payments. Once you are there, you simply follow the process outlined by selecting the amount of the payment, the frequency of the payment, and the payment method that you would like to use.

This option may also be better for things like credit cards that may not always have a balance that you are paying towards. If there is no balance due on your credit card account, and you have recurring payments scheduled, then no payment will be pulled for that payment cycle.

This is one of my favorite ways to stay on top of my bills as I can schedule micropayments to come out each pay period versus trying to pay a bill in full when it is due. I save money on interest in the future because I can pay down more of the principal on my account by making payments slightly above the minimum amount due. And I can do this while not feeling like I am spending all my money on bills at one time as the payments are broken up into smaller and more manageable amounts.

For someone who absolutely hates to feel broke two

days after payday, this is a lifesaver of a method as you do not have those giant payments coming out when you get paid! You get to space out the total amount due over a seemingly longer period of time and give yourself peace of mind that your bills will be paid on time and you don't have to worry about anything!

NEGOTIATE YOUR BILLS

One more piece of advice that is related to your bills is to negotiate service prices if you can. Some service providers start you out at an introductory price for one, two, or even three years. Then, they go in and up your service price once that time frame has passed. If you have a solid payment history with them for the entire introductory period, however, you may be able to call the service provider and ask for a lower price on the service, especially if you are unable to afford the service at the new higher price. If they say they are unable to adjust the price and you cannot afford the higher rate, then it would be best to advise them that you will need to downgrade your plan or cancel your service. Sometimes, this threat of losing a customer will also have them suddenly "able to find a lower price point for you". I have seen this happen personally a few different times. I called a service provider because I no longer needed the service. It was not being used as often in my home as needed to justify the cost and I had planned to just cancel to cut back on my spending. However, the rep on the phone informed me that they would be able to switch me over to another plan being offered that was a quarter of the price that I was currently paying. So that means I could keep the service that I occasionally used and still have decent savings each month.

And I am not advising lying to your service provider to get a cheaper service. If they tell you that they cannot negotiate your service price, then you need to personally evaluate if the service is necessary and if it is affordable at the current price. If it is not necessary, then you should probably cancel anyway. If the service is necessary but not affordable, then you should research other service providers before speaking to your current service provider about negotiating a new price. Sometimes, service providers will price match to avoid losing a customer to another provider. Or maybe, when you researching new providers, you will find one who is offering a much better inclusive package at a lower rate and truly want to switch.

It is never a bad thing to talk with your service provider about pricing. The worst they can do is say that they cannot negotiate. This is another situation though where you want to make sure that you have made on-time payments every month for your service. If you have a history of late payments, the provider may not be willing to work with you.

CLEAR YOUR DEBT... ASAP!

This one is one that really rings true for me. I have consistently been in debt for much of my adult life. Starting with traditional student loans, adding on credit cards, car payments, house payments, and many other things. And like a lot of people, I was not always aware of the best ways to manage my debt and repayments. So, a lot of my accounts made it to….

COLLECTIONS.

Ugh, even the thought of that word gives me a nervous feeling. Seeing that new collections account pop up on your credit report is always a punch in the gut.

Did you know that having collections accounts showing up on your credit report makes it nearly impossible to improve your credit score? The negative impact on your credit from an account in collections is so great that your on-time payment history and responsible use of open credit accounts are not able to make much, if any, impact month after month.

My fiancé and I were trying to look into buying a house last year. We were coming up on the end of our previous lease and needed to find something new. Rent prices are out of control so we decided to look into buying our first house together.

My fiancé has never owned a home at this point. He has always rented. So, he was new to the process and kind of sat back and let me do my thing (props to this guy for dealing with me and my set-in-stone ways!). He does not have the blemishes on his credit history that I do.

As I mentioned much earlier, I previously owned a home that I lost due to foreclosure. It had been over three years since then, so I knew that the foreclosure would no longer adversely affect my application for a new mortgage.

What I did not know until I spoke with a mortgage advisor was that the outstanding collections accounts on my credit report from years prior were still dragging down my credit score. This stopped us from being able to obtain a new mortgage loan. We had to find another rental that we could afford, which was a huge accomplishment on our budget. A mortgage payment would have been much cheaper than renting something that would never be ours and that we could not decorate freely as we wanted. The mortgage advisor that I spoke with suggested paying off my collections accounts and was the person who educated me on the severity of the impact they have on your credit score. They explained that with open collections accounts, other factors just do not have enough weight to change anything. And they advised that by removing even one of my collection accounts, I could see a nice increase in my credit score that would have bumped me over the threshold of eligibility for a new mortgage loan.

It was a defeating moment for a little while to know that my old debt from years prior was stopping us from moving forward together.

And then I realized that I did not need to see it that way. Instead, I decided to look at it as an inspiration and motivation to work a little harder and do a little more for us. When the situation arises again where we are looking at new housing options, my credit will no longer be a stopping point for us because I decided to make sure I changed it for the better.

So, what can you do if you have accounts in collections already? You've got your normal bills and costs of living. Your expenses are stretched kind of thin at this point. How do you go about paying off those collection accounts so you can recover your credit score and let it work for you? The simple answer is you pay as you can by following the auto payment method that we discussed for bills.

If you have decided that you are ready to pay off those collections accounts, then you need to contact the creditor/collection agency and request a written verification of the debt, along with options on how to make payments if the debt is verified to be yours. You can also ask them to send information on deals for repayment if you feel like the total is going to be something you will never be able to repay.

Just be careful how you speak to the creditor/collection agency. Never, NEVER, accept responsibility for the debt over the phone on your initial communication. Make it clear that you are first and foremost requesting a verification of the debt. I know this is something you have probably had drilled in your head a few hundred times, but it is actually a very important step. If you accept responsibility for the debt over the phone, the creditor/collection agency can immediately begin taking other action to recover the debt. If you request verification of the debt, then all collection efforts must be stopped for a certain period of time, giving you time to review the debt and make a plan for payment moving forward.

Once you have received this information from the creditor, you need to make a plan. Based on the information that they sent to you, is there an amount that you could comfortably pay every so often to start working on reducing the balance of the debt? Can you afford $10 a week to pay off the debt? $25? $50?

When you are making this repayment plan, always remember to use the snowball method for repaying debt. Let's say you have four accounts in collections. One account has a balance of $300, one is $950, one is $450, and one is $145. You would want to get verifications for all your debt, and then start making incremental payments on each. Once the smallest one is paid off you put that extra amount you were paying towards the next smallest account. Continue in this fashion and you can repay all your collections in no time!

To continue with our example accounts, let's say you decide that you can afford to pay $25 a week on each account, so $100 a week total. Well, after six weeks, your smallest account (with a starting balance of $145) will be paid off. So now, instead of $25 a week, you can make a payment of $50 per week on your account that originally had a balance of $300. This means in just three more weeks you will have your second account paid off. And now you can add that extra $50 per week to the payment on the $450 dollar account (which at week nine would have a remaining balance of $225). Exactly three more weeks and that account is paid in full. You can now pay $100 per week on the account that had the largest balance. This will allow you to pay off your final account in just six more weeks.

So, in this example, we went from $1,795 in collections to $0 in collections in just eighteen weeks, or approximately four and a half months!! And you will have that extra $100 per week that you were using to pay on your accounts to put back into your savings or fun fund!

By the way, did I mention that once you pay your accounts in full (or as agreed upon with the creditor/collection agency) that they will report that information to the credit bureaus? This means that as soon as you pay off your first account, you could start seeing your score increase. Please keep in mind that the creditors/collection agencies may take their sweet time reporting this to the credit bureaus so you may not see any change for thirty days or more after you make the final payment on the account. They may also report this information differently depending on the repayment arrangement that you agreed to with them.

For example, if your total account due was for $1,500 but you and the creditor agreed that the debt would be cleared if you paid back $900 of the debt, then the creditor may code the cleared debt in a different method. Instead of saying that the account was "paid in full", it may be reported as "paid in full as agreed upon". I am not a credit expert, so I cannot say what the difference in impact will be to a credit score. But I would definitely suggest making sure that you know exactly how the payoff will be reported by the creditor before you enter into a payment arrangement with them. Then you can do your own research as to how the reporting can affect your score on based on reports from an average number of people.

These steps may seem scary at first, but once you get started, I promise it becomes much easier to comprehend. And you do not have to start payments on all of your credit accounts at once! You could reach out to just one or two creditors to start and then reach out to another one or two once you are close to hitting a payoff date for the first account(s). This may make it easier to fit in payments starting out if you do not have a lot to spare and want to work on paying off just a small amount of debt at a time.

Now. this may cause the process to take a little longer since you would not be paying on all your accounts from the start. In the end, you need to use your own judgment on the best approach for you and your own situation. For me, smaller payments spread out across all my accounts from the start is the best method. Others may want to make slightly larger payments on half of their accounts to start. And others may want to pay on one account at a time.

Any of these, or any other methods you may find on your own, are the right method! Find what works for you and get started on it as soon as you can. Watching your debt fall off is an amazing feeling and will open up more opportunities for you in the future as your credit score goes higher and higher! New home loan options, business loan options, credit cards, and car loans. Once you clear that debt, you will really have unlimited ways to move forward!

TO SPEND OR NOT TO SPEND

Now we are going to discuss spending. More specifically, not spending. The best advice for this is: do not spend everything you make. Seems pretty simple and self-explanatory right? But you may be asking "Well how do I keep from spending my whole paycheck with having bills, groceries, household essentials, collections payments, and more?".

If you are looking for an easy answer to this: I'm sorry because there isn't one.

What I can tell you is: cutback but do it in a way that does not feel like cutting back. Do not set such a strict budget for yourself that you start feeling like you no longer have a life or anything for yourself. This will give you a very adverse reaction as far as your happiness level and you may start feeling anxious, depressed, or even suffocated by the fact that you can no longer go out and do things.

Try implementing the "Need It, Want It, What Is It" method. Look at the item you are wanting to purchase. Is it something that you truly need? If not a need, then is it something that you want and have wanted for a very long time?

If you answered 'No' to both of these questions, then the item falls into the 'What is it' category. This means it is not a necessity and is not even something that you have been wanting. This may be an impulse buy because you saw it on a shelf in the store or you were scrolling through Amazon and saw this thing that you feel like you want right now. Items in this category should be put on hold! Take a picture of the item if you are physically in the store. Save it to a list or add it to your 'Saved for Later' items if you came across it while online shopping. Then, seriously think about the item. Check out the features. Read reviews. See if you can find it at a better price somewhere else. And, most importantly, decide if it is something that will make your life any better.

Having impulse purchase control is a difficult skill to master. I still struggle with it to this day. But I am much better than I was ten, or even five, years ago. Because I practice this skill all the time.

My fiancé, on the other hand, is amazing at this, and always has been! He does thorough research on any item he is considering purchasing that is out of the norm for him and not something that he needs. He seriously weighs the benefits of the item against the cost and decides if it is worth it to him. And a lot of the time, he decides not to buy.

But we both allow ourselves the grace of occasionally breaking this rule and purchasing something on impulse just because we feel that we really want it. Cutting back. Impulse control. It is all a balancing act. You have to hold off on some occasions and allow yourself to splurge on others.

You are the only person who can truly set a limit on what you spend or don't spend. You know your situation better than anyone else. And you know your shopping habits. Looking at those habits and seeing what you can, or are willing, to trim is a decision you must make for yourself.

SO, HOW DO I START CUTTING BACK?

Any cutbacks you can implement will allow you to start saving right off the bat with no wait time at all. This means immediately being able to build up your savings and your emergency cushion. This is one of the easiest, fastest, and admittedly smartest ways to prepare yourself for the worst-case scenario.

Choose a cheaper brand, or store brand, when you can. You'd be amazed at how well those knockoffs work. There is nothing wrong with sticking to a name brand if nothing else hits the mark either (I am a stickler for certain brands in mac & cheese and dish detergent myself). But a lot of off-brand cleaners are highly competitive with big brand names currently. I absolutely love trying something that is cheaper and realizing it works the same or better as its competitor for under half the price!

In the case where downgrading on brand is not

an option, then maybe consider buying a smaller amount instead of buying in bulk. You can find some great deals on items from large brand names in smaller packaging. You can also find good sales on two-for-ones with smaller package offerings.

While you can sometimes get a better deal in the long run with buying in bulk, you need to also consider if you are using everything that you purchase, or if you are having to throw things out. If you are buying in bulk and tossing some of what you buy, then that is money literally being thrown in the trash. If that is the case, then downsize your purchase. And keep downsizing until you find an amount where you have almost zero waste. If you find yourself frequently buying the same item and always throwing some out, then maybe think about cutting the purchase of the item altogether if possible.

One example of this is those little dental flosser picks. I was consistent about buying the big bags of these because I know my fiancé liked to have them around "just in case". However, more often than not, I would end up throwing out over half a bag because we never used them up. He would opt for a regular toothpick from the kitchen, or the bag would fall over and spill into the sink. Whatever the reason, they just were not getting used up. So, I stopped buying them. Turns out, he does fine with regular toothpicks, and I can save a few bucks a month!

Next, that high-end retailer that you swear by or the retailer that you are comfortable with but you know they overcharge on almost every item compared to other retailers? Drop them for everything but the items you cannot find anywhere else.

I used to shop religiously at one large grocery retailer. I could make one stop and get absolutely everything I needed! They also used to have a wonderful savings program that they have since eliminated that would get you money back on any purchase that was advertised cheaper at another retailer. However, I eventually realized that without that savings initiative, I was spending more money than I would at another grocer. I made the switch for all food purchases and have never regretted the decision!

I have always been a fan of 'dollar stores'. And it does not matter which one. Any of them, all of them. They are wonderful for finding things you use regularly for a better price. Check out their $1 section as well! You would be amazed at what you can still find for just $1 that you probably use pretty frequently without realizing it!

I recently started a personal experiment within my own life to see how many items I could start buying at Dollar Tree versus buying the same giant name brand or high-end products I had previously used. I started with simple supplies like pens, paper, plasticware, and such. Then I moved to cleaning supplies, food items, bathroom supplies, and even makeup. Yes, I really said that I have started buying my makeup at Dollar Tree. And guess what? I have found some amazing products that I will continue to buy even when I no longer need to (including the best foundation I have ever used)!

The point here is that if you cut some of the excess spending you do on a daily or weekly basis, you will have more money out of each check. And why is that important? More money not being spent means more savings. More savings means more cushion if you suddenly find yourself out of a job.

Now, should you go cold turkey and cut your spending across the board and stop having fun? Absolutely not! This will only cause you to feel stuck and like you are never able to do anything. As I mentioned before, this will be completely counter-productive to the goal which is to make sure you are better prepared for the worst-case scenario. And if you are anything like me, eventually you will get so tired of never doing anything that you go on a spending bender and blow through a lot of your savings without even blinking.

Talk about bad ideas!

So how do you balance cutbacks and spending so that you still feel like you can do little extras for yourself? Incremental cutbacks and savings. Only minor changes.

Do not, I repeat, DO NOT go extravagant with cutbacks at first!

If you fall off the wagon or give in to temptations to spend, you will be less likely to keep going. Starting out small significantly lowers the chance of slipping and feeling like you cannot stick to your plan. Just start small and celebrate every little save. Make sure that you still do things for yourself as well. Just because you cut back does not mean that every penny saved must go into your savings.

REAL-LIFE SCENARIOS FOR CUTBACKS

Do you like getting your nails done at the salon? Try adding an extra week between fill-ins or new sets. One extra week may add a little extra nail growth but won't make your nails hideous by the time you get them redone. Or get super adventurous and try doing your own artificials at home! I know, I know, all the salon owners and patrons reading this are probably screaming inside, however, occasionally doing your own nails could save you a massive amount of money in the long run. Dip powder kits are excellent if you want low-maintenance color and are not worried about extra length. And there are artificial tip kits available all over now where you can build out your nails to the length you want, all without ever getting out of your PJs, putting gas in your car, and paying for a service and tip!

Instead of the super-inclusive barbershop package

with the hot towel shave, try doing it yourself at home every other time. Do your own hair trims. If you are feeling super brave, do your own color as well! I can attest to the fact that there is nothing better than the feeling when you nail the color you were going for and you know that you did it by yourself!

I had my fiancé do my hair color for me on my last birthday. And we went all out! I got foils (which, by the way, I had never done myself, let alone had him do!), multiple color creams and developers, hair bonnets for the processing time, and a couple of brushes and bowls. All these supplies cost me less than it would have to go out and have a professional color my hair. And guess what?

My fiancé rocked the color for me!

He perfectly layered my highlighted sections all throughout my hair so that when we finished the process (about four hours later!) you would have thought I just stepped out of a salon, for about a quarter of the price! Even better, we had so much fun laughing together in the bathroom while he worked on my hair!! I never would have thought that would be an activity we would do to spend time together, but I am so glad now that we did!

Go out to dinner occasionally. Fast food, sit down, whatever your preference. Just go out and have someone else cook your meal and clean up after. Fit in a meal out to feel a little luxurious from time to time without breaking the bank. Skip the expensive drinks and crack open a cheap bottle of wine when you get home. Dessert too. Make your own dessert to have ready to go and it will be much more enjoyable and cheaper. As a bonus, you will have more servings if you make your own full-size dessert instead of ordering at a restaurant. So, you will get to enjoy it multiple times. Win-win!

One of the most fun date ideas out there is to dress up really snazzy and go somewhere silly for a night out, like McDonald's. Just go all out with a fancy dress, high heels, a tux, some nice loafers, etc. And then go grab a burger and some fries and chow down! It can be such a freeing experience to dress to the nines and then go somewhere that you don't have to act a certain type of way. Plus, the "I wonder who that couple is" looks that you get from other restaurant patrons never gets old!!

For any of my fellow coffee addicts out there, this one is a hard one for me. But if you can do it then you will definitely see some extra dough piling up. I am absolutely addicted to my McDonald's Iced Caramel Coffee. I have them add some caramel drizzle and whipped cream (and a shot of espresso if it is still really early in the morning) and they are delicious! However, I was averaging three or four of these coffees a day, at over $2 a pop. Meaning I was spending almost $10 per day on coffee, or close to $70 per week! Not to mention I would grab my fiancé a $5 latte or americano as well each day.

Yikes!!

That just bumped my spending to over $100 per week on coffee! So, I simply made myself stop going in the mornings. I cleaned off our dusty old coffee pot and started making myself a pot of hot water each day. I found a brand of instant coffee that I really enjoy (from Dollar Tree no less!). Then I found a sugar-free creamer that I adore! And voila!! I am now spending only $5 per week on my own coffee! Don't worry, my fiancé found some instant espresso that he enjoys as well (about $5 for a jar that will last him two or three weeks) so he does not have to go without coffee because I decided to cut back.

We still occasionally go through and grab one of our faves from McD's as a treat. But we are saving a ridiculous amount of money each week by doing just that. Using high-end coffees as a treat and not a staple.

I know this seems impossible to some of you. It did to me too. And trust me it was not easy, for me or my fiancé. There were times when I would be craving an iced coffee so badly that I would just give in and go at first. It took some patience to find the right mix in my homemade coffee to keep me from wanting to run uptown and place that order. But I found the right recipe for me and now I am saving a boatload of money each month.

The point is to spend money on yourself while still saving money overall. Keep yourself feeling as if you are not missing out and you will be much more likely to be able to save money. This will get you set up in the proper way to be secure and not have to scramble and accept the first offer you receive should the time come when you are needing to look for a new job.

COUPONING? FOR REAL?

Yes! Couponing is alive and well, and is much easier than you might think. When I say that you should start couponing, I am not talking about going extreme as you see on TV. I am talking about starting simple with things you already buy anyway. When you are thinking about eating out, use coupons and mobile apps for savings. McDonald's is one that has daily deals on discounted or even free items through their mobile app, and they give out rewards points on all orders that you can redeem for free items as well! I know many other restaurants have implemented this same type of offer system in their own mobile apps, including Burger King, Dominos, Pizza Hut, Arby's, and more.

Also, do not throw away the weekly flyers with the restaurant inserts that have paper coupons in them. Maybe you don't use a restaurant's mobile app, but you still go occasionally. These paper coupons are a great way to cut back on your spending when eating out without much extra work. Just take a look at your coupons before you head out and see if anything looks good. Then bring the coupon along with you! It is that easy!

You should definitely check with your retailer and see if they offer any type of savings program as well. A lot of major retailers, like Wal-Mart and Kroger, have started implementing different rewards subscriptions, digital offers, and other things. Digital coupons for retailers are my favorite because you clip them from the app, put your phone number in at checkout, and watch your total start dropping! I have saved as much as $50 in one shopping trip with a retailer's digital coupons!! I treated myself to an iced coffee after shopping and threw the rest into my savings!

You don't absolutely have to have a coupon ready for every purchase that you make, but if you take just a few minutes each week to look through the retailers' sites that you frequent, you may be able to find some really good deals on things that you were already going to purchase. I have even used a coupon as a reason to try a new brand or item entirely instead of something else that I would normally buy. This has led to me finding some new favorites!

SUBSCRIPTION FEES BE GONE!

More than likely, you have multiple subscriptions active already. Amazon Prime, Netflix, Hulu, Disney +, Xbox Live, Splendies, Ipsy, Birchbox, Barkbox, Chewy, etc. These can be very easily downsized. And you should not notice much of a difference once you do it.

For example, if you have four different streaming services active right now, just cutting that in half will save you a bundle! And you will start seeing those savings in the very next billing cycle.

Another great idea centered around streaming services is having them bundled with another product that you already purchase. My cell phone carrier offers a service plan that comes with free access to a streaming service. This means I have a streaming account ready to go just for having something I was already going to be paying for.

There is no extra fee for the streaming service either. It is included in the regular cost of my service.

When you are considering what streaming services you want to keep, there are three questions you should ask yourself to make it an easy decision. Is there something that you consistently watch that you cannot watch anywhere else? Have you already watched it a hundred times? Are there still new episodes being made and released?

If your answers were no, yes, and no, it is time to ditch the extra subscription!

Are you someone like me who loves getting mystery boxes? I love, love, LOVE Ipsy, Splendies, and Birchbox!! And if I were at a point where I was comfortable with my savings cushion, I may subscribe to one or two of them again. However, knowing that I need to work on building my savings, I decided to stop all my box subscriptions until I have more cushion for the future.

Because, while getting surprise boxes every month is awesome and I love trying new products, I love stability even more. If I am feeling luxurious, I can shop for one new product to try myself instead of having a whole box of new products show up every month, with no guarantee that I will like all, or even any, of the products that I am being sent.

The same goes for items for your pets. If you are getting a subscription box for your pet but you feel like you need to be saving money, cut that subscription ASAP! Your pet will understand if they only get one new toy or container of treats every so often versus a whole box of stuff. And I promise, they will still love you just as much!

It is another major decision to consider if you truly need whatever item you are subscribed to and does it improve your life at this moment. Or does it take resources away from other things that matter more in the right now? Do not cut so many items at once that you feel deprived, but make sure you are not losing hundreds of dollars each month on subscriptions that you do not use or truly see a value in.

SETTING UP YOUR SAVINGS TO WORK FOR YOU

So, you have managed to start working on a few of these items and now you have extra money that you did not have before. What do you do with it?

My number one suggestion? Make it work for you!

Meaning, put it into a savings account or investment account of some type so that it earns you more money without you having to lift a finger! An added perk of these extra savings is being able to achieve your short and long-term goals more easily.

Trying to save for a deposit on a bigger apartment or a down payment on a new home or car? Break up your savings into multiple accounts with different interest rates based on what the savings will be for (i.e., short-term, long-term, or an emergency fund). You could search your phone's app store to see if you can find a new banking/investment app to set up additional accounts just for saving.

There are tons of apps out there that offer different features for small monthly account maintenance fees or even for free. In my opinion, several of the apps with maintenance fees have benefits that far outweigh the fees. Having these apps means you can also set up automatic transfers from your standard account that receives your direct deposit to the app to grow your savings without thinking about it.

These apps that connect directly to your standard accounts can have additional features automatically integrated with your bank account to discover additional ways to save. One of my favorite apps has about four different savings features that you can add on and customize to meet your own savings goals. There are features for round up savings (rounds up each purchase you make and moves the savings to your app account on a specific day each week), set and forget saving (you pick an amount to have moved on a specific day each week), cash back (you choose from a list of retailers and receive automatic cashback into your savings app each week), and there is even a fine feature.

With this feature, you choose a certain retailer that you are trying not to shop at as much. Every time a purchase comes through for that retailer, the app takes the amount of money that you designate and sets it up to move on a specific day. Kind of like a penalty charge for shopping at the location where you are trying to cutback but the money charged goes into your own savings account!

There are even features designed to smart save for you. This feature is great because the app looks at your deposit and spending activity for the week. It also examines your balance. Then, based on your own income and spending habits, the app designates a certain amount of money each week to be transferred over to your savings account. This amount can fluctuate each week based on income and spending changes, and can even be somewhat customized by choosing if you would like a chill savings plan (meaning not as much will be calculated to leave a greater cushion in your spending account) or an aggressive savings plan (meaning the app will calculate a larger smart save each week and not leave as much of a spend cushion).

Another feature to look for is actual investment capability. There are tons of apps on the market now that let you use your savings to invest in the stock market without needing to be an expert. You could loosely compare them to a 401k account with the fact that you can schedule transfers into these accounts and the funds can be auto-invested into different stock and bond options that you personally select or based on a selected pre-built investment plan. You can usually choose how risky you would like to be in your investments (meaning you select which type of accounts your money will be invested into, like stocks, bonds, etc.). This is a feature that could result in great growth of your savings over time and allow you to have a nice cushion if the time would come when you really need the money.

But wait. Maybe you don't want to create a new account through an app or another bank. You love your current banking institution and do not want to put any of your money elsewhere. See if your bank has a round-up savings option. This is an awesome type of savings feature available with a lot of banks that will automatically round up all purchases made with your debit card and move the change over to a savings account.

Saving without having to think about it! What more could you want?!

Check with your bank (or do some searching on your online or mobile banking platform) and see if your checking and savings accounts support transfer from one account to the other. If your accounts allow this, consider setting up an automatic transfer from your checking to your standard savings account, based on the amount of extra money you have on hand each week (or each pay period in case you are not paid weekly). Or even see if you can create a secondary savings account that could have a better interest rate for longer-term savings ans start auto transfers into one or both of your accounts!

Let's say that you started doing some cutbacks and saving an extra $20 per week. You want to keep access to $10 in case you want to grab that extra coffee while you are out, but you would like to move the other $10 to your savings. And you know that this is an amount you can consistently move over without having it affect your ability to pay your bills and get what you need to live.

Then you can use the auto-transfer feature offered by your bank to move that $10 over each week without even having to think about it! I usually schedule all my automatic bill payments and savings transfers for the business day after my payday so that I know that the funds will be in my account and available for use. This is another way for me to be able to set up my savings without having to worry about anything getting in the way!

HAVE A FRIEND...
OR TWO!

We have talked quite a bit so far about the things you can do that revolve around money. But are there other things you can change outside of money? Absolutely! The first thing is to have a friend.

Now, I do not mean a touch base occasionally type of friend. I mean a good friend that you are in consistent communication with. Stay connected. Text at least every couple of days. Call a couple of times a week. Make sure you engage in their life, and they are involved in yours.

Also, make sure your friend is not also your spouse or romantic partner. Yes, your spouse is a great support system and always should be. But an outside friend will also be truthful with you if you mess up or if you need to work on something. A spouse, on the other hand, may tell you everything is perfect the way it is because they love you and they truly do not believe that anything needs to change.

You need an unbiased opinion if you get into a rough situation and need to start looking for a new role. This is going to give you an added support system as well. This will be an extra shoulder to lean on for emotional support.

If your friend happens to be in the same industry as you, they will add extra value in this type of situation as well. They will be able to offer insight and guidance into the industry and where you can begin your search and help you when you start feeling stuck. If you have more than one friend, even better! They can offer different perspectives based on their own knowledge and experiences.

Keep your support system in place and you will make it through the roughest patches without adding too many scars.

STOP SCROLLING SOCIAL MEDIA AND FIND A REAL HOBBY!

Wait a minute, Brooke, I thought you said to network on LinkedIn?

Yep, I sure did!

But there is a significant difference between LinkedIn and most other social media platforms out there. LinkedIn is a professional site. While you do see the occasional post about something personal that happened to someone, most of the content on LinkedIn is created by professionals for professionals.

I, myself, do not truly consider LinkedIn social media as it is a professional tool that has even been required to be used in my career.

For the most part, what do you see when you scroll through other social media platforms? Is it anything of substance? Do you see life-changing posts? Is there anything on there that affects you directly? Or is most of what you see status bragging posts or posts of people whining about things that happened to them that, in the grand scheme of things, are not even that bad? Or pictures of old friends that you do not even speak to besides the occasional like or comment on something one or the other of you shares?

I personally made the choice to cut out standard social media over a year ago. And I can easily say I am so much happier without it! All of that wasted time spent scrolling through the feed just so I could compare myself to other people posting about things that did or had.

How sad is that?

So now, I use those extra hours each day to read a new book (wonder where I got the idea to write one?). I have always loved to crochet and so I recently taught myself knitting as well. And once I moved into Technical Recruiting, I decided I wanted to be as knowledgeable as possible, and so I started doing online courses on coding in Python.

I have picked up how-to guides in several areas, including programming, business process management, and more. And my collection of fiction novels has grown tremendously.

And guess what?

I do not miss the feed scrolling one bit! I check my LinkedIn a couple of times per day, but I usually spend no more than ten or fifteen minutes at a time on the site. And much of that time is spent applying for jobs, posting new content to my page, or sending new connection requests to people in my industry. There really is no absent-minded scrolling to be done.

If you remove the pressure from yourself of consistently looking at other people posting about their gains in life, you will be better able to see what is so great about your own life just the way that it is! Do not compare yourself to anyone else, especially through something like social media where the majority of people only post positives anyway and there is a biased lens through which you would be viewing these posts.

Find something that you really love doing and fill the time gaps that you used to spend scrolling. At first, you will probably instinctively pick up your phone throughout the day to start scrolling (I know I did!). But your mind will eventually reset from this habit and instead will drift to the new hobby that you have picked up. Bonus points if your new hobby lets you keep learning while you do it (remember my tip from preparing for the worst?)!

EXERCISE AND THE VALUE IT GIVES

Are you the type of person that rolls your eyes when someone starts discussing that you should exercise your brains out?

I absolutely am!

I cannot stand listening to people go on and on about how everybody has to exercise because of this and that. A lot of fitness guides will preach about setting up your routines and you can't miss a day and blah, blah, blah. While these types of people tend to annoy me a bit (sorry guys, but I am an honest person and don't want to lie), they do make some good points.

Do you have to exercise every day? Nope, definitely not.

Do you have to exercise every other day? Nope, definitely not.

But should you get up and exercise at least

occasionally? Yes, absolutely!

I am someone who has been very overweight for most of my life. But I do not exercise to lose weight. I exercise for ease of breathing. I exercise to clear my mind. I exercise to take out my life frustrations in a productive way.

That is the wonderful thing about exercise. It gives you a free outlet in an almost unlimited number of methods. You can walk, jog, or run. You can bike. You can do shadowboxing (super fun by the way!). You can roller skate or skateboard. You can jump rope. And a million other things that would take too long to list.

Now, obviously, from my previous statements, I am not an exercise queen. I DO NOT set an exercise schedule for myself. From my own previous experience, making an exercise schedule was a surefire way for me to never stick with it. If I felt like I absolutely had to exercise because it was set in my schedule, then it did not feel as fun to me.

And that is the most important thing to remember about exercise.

You should enjoy it!

Exercising just to say you exercise will not accomplish anything. The exercise that you do should provide value to your life. It should make you feel good. It should give you a way to de-stress your life. And it should not feel like work.

Now I am not saying that you should not push yourself when you are exercising. You should always try to come up with new highs or personal bests to reach. But you should be setting these new goals to be reasonable and something that would give you a sense of accomplishment. You should not be setting goals that will feel unattainable and make you feel defeated when you are trying to reach them.

My exercise comes from moving about my home during the day, cleaning, and then walking anywhere in town that I need to go. I do not add in any additional exercise at this time in my life because I feel that my days are very full, and I do not want to overload myself with additional tasks to do that are not necessary for me to survive and be happy. But I will push myself to walk further than before.

For example, I decided to walk to a store at the opposite end of town from where I live instead of walking to the closest store to my home. I had a day where the weather was really nice, and I wanted to be out longer and push myself a bit to see if I could walk the distance to that store and back.

I am sure you know that as you get older, it gets harder to go as far. Your stamina will decrease. Your breathing gets more labored. This is especially true if you have gained a bunch of weight as I have over the past few years. And I will be the first to tell you I am massively out of shape.

So, an added benefit of walking everywhere in town right now is that I am rebuilding my stamina. And now when my fiancé and I take our walks through town, we can go farther without my lungs feeling like they are shredding.

The whole point is that you should be incorporating some exercise into your life. Make it something that you find fun. If you do this, you won't feel like it is 'exercise' and you will be more likely to keep doing it and using it as an outlet for stress and such. But you also should not let yourself feel bad if you skip a day, or even a week, of exercise.

YOU HAVE TO REST AND REPEAT

One of the biggest ways to take care of yourself is by resting. Regardless of what else you have going on in your life, you must allow yourself the chance to recharge. You cannot keep yourself going at 100% all the time. This would cause you to burn out, at work and at home.

Your version of rest and my version of rest could be very different. For me, resting means sitting up in my bed in the evenings and doing a few more rows on my current knitting project while one of my favorite shows plays on the TV in the background. I can sit back and zone out while keeping my hands busy and my mind semi-occupied.

When I am resting, I do not like to be bored. And just sitting and watching TV alone can be very boring to me, regardless of what I may be watching. I like to have an activity to do while I am watching my shows. I do not like for my mind to fully slow down. So, I will do my craft work, play an idle game on my phone, or even do a crossword puzzle or two. Other people may like to completely slow themselves down and just read a book or watch a movie while doing nothing else.

You have to find the way that you prefer to rest where there are no expectations, and nothing is required from you. Maybe you are like me and want to stay busy but not have anything you are feeling pushed to do. Maybe you like to veg out on the sofa or take a three-hour nap. Either way, rest the way you want and keep your internal battery full!

COMMITMENT IS KEY

Whenever you come up with a new plan, it requires commitment. Just like every other aspect of your life, happiness requires commitment too. You have to make a choice every single day to be happy, regardless of what circumstances you may be facing. Does that mean that you cannot experience other feelings like anger, sadness, or exhaustion? No, it most definitely does not.

What it does mean is that while you may temporarily have those feelings, you must commit to having an overall happy life. If you are implementing tips to make your life genuinely happier, then, when you encounter a situation that makes you sad, you will be better equipped to handle your sadness and move back into feeling happy.

Commitment carries through for each piece of advice given in this guide.

Wanting to cut back on spending? You need to commit!

Wanting to grow your savings? You need to commit!

Trying to increase your marketability by doing

certification courses? You must commit!

There is a different level of commitment needed in each of these scenarios. For a certification course, for example, you need to commit to finishing the course and understanding the material needed to pass your certification test. For cutting back on spending, you have to commit each and every day not to do impulse spending.

But you also have to be willing to commit to forgiving yourself. You will slip up. You will make mistakes. You may set a goal of saving $50 per week and still have a week where you go $75 over budget. Give yourself some grace and allow yourself to recommit to cutting back the following week. Know that you are only human, and we all make mistakes and mess up. And sometimes, we all have trouble keeping our commitments.

The biggest thing is to just commit to bettering yourself, in any and every way. Make that commitment the most important in your life and all the other commitments will fall in line with that. You can make as many plans as you want. But just remember if you are unable to stick to them for any reason that it is not the end of the world. It does not make you a failure. It does not define you in any kind of way.

PART IV – THE WRAP-UP

WHAT ARE THE TAKEAWAYS

The message of this guide is simple.

Keep growing folks!

That's it. The entire message boiled down to one sentence.

The steps for achieving this are simple. Spend less, save more, and do things that make you happy, while consistently building your knowledge and skills.

The entire point of this guide is to help you see that you do not need someone else to dictate your level of happiness. You can easily make changes to your own life that will increase the value you see in yourself while making sure that you are prepared in case something negative happens in the future, like a layoff.

With these steps, you will have a higher level of happiness and a greater level of preparedness. So, if

the worst does happen, it will not break you. It will be an opportunity for you to rise and showcase your self-built strengths and abilities!
So, what are you waiting for?
The guide is done, now go make some changes and live a happier life!

ABOUT THE AUTHOR

Brooke Barnes

Brooke Barnes is a regular person. She does not have a long list of awards and accolades. She does not hold a degree. She spent most of her life in the Hillsboro, Ohio area. She now lives in Greenfield, Ohio with her fiancé, Scott Pearson. They have four children together. 

Brooke has made her career as an HR and Recruiting professional. She truly enjoys helping people find the place that they belong in their careers, as well as helping to resolve any issues they may encounter while working.

Brooke is an avid reader. She also enjoys crafts (usually crocheting or knitting), thrift shopping, and spending time with her family.